BUILDING BRIDGES

THE CASE FOR EXECUTIVE
PEER NETWORKS

JAMES MILLAR

First published in 2018 by SkyBridge Associates, LLC
Copyright © James Millar 2018

Hardback ISBN 978-1-7322826-0-5

Also available in paperback
ISBN 978-1-7322826-1-2

And as an ebook
978-1-7322826-2-9

Library of Congress Control Number: 2018906279

Designed and typeset by k-design.org.uk
Cover design by Alice Moore

For more information, please contact
buildingbridges@skybridge.associates.

CONTENTS

INTRODUCTION

I N MAY 1974, a 26-year-old named Jon Landau attended a concert at a small theater in Cambridge, Massachusetts. After the show, he famously wrote in a local publication:

> *I saw rock and roll future and its name is Bruce Springsteen. And on a night when I needed to feel young, he made me feel like I was hearing music for the very first time.*

Landau went on to become Springsteen's manager and producer, and that 1974 show almost certainly changed both their lives.

This short book is not about music or Bruce Springsteen, though both have an important place in my heart. Rather, this is about passion, curiosity, and a quest to draw on diverse influences to help others see things for the very first time too.

Several years after their first meeting, Landau described Springsteen as a paradox:

Bruce is a man with a vision and at the same time, he's in search of a vision.

I understand what it's like to have both a vision and a restless need to refine that vision. I wrote this short book to share my vision with executives who seek deeper connections with peers, clients, and other important stakeholders. We will explore not just *how* executives can create and sustain richer peer networks, but also *why* these relationships are so important.

WHO AM I?

Let me introduce myself. I was born in Toronto in 1965 and spent most of the first 23 years of my life in Canada before moving to the United States after college. I have an engineering degree, but started my professional career in investment banking, as a financial analyst at Morgan Stanley. This two-year program was an excellent introduction to business, and it paved the way to Harvard Business School. When I graduated with my MBA in 1992, I decided to forego the typical Wall Street and management consulting jobs to join the Harvard MBA Admissions Board. This was a good move for me, and I learned a lot over the next seven years about what makes leaders tick!

I left HBS in 1999 and worked in a couple marketing and entrepreneurial roles before I finally found my calling. Since 2004, I have been creating and leading elite, invitation-only executive networks—private clubs for peers who should be talking regularly with each other but aren't. It's fun, challenging, and creative work, which allows me to draw on all the insights, experiences, and skills I have gained over the course of my career.

WHY ARE GREAT PEER NETWORKS SO VALUABLE—AND SO RARE?

I have a recurring memory, and I can't shake it. I was standing on a top floor of a midtown Manhattan office tower, chatting with a network member after a three-hour roundtable meeting. He asked about our firm's growth plans. Suddenly, it all became clear. "Look out the window," I suggested. "There are hundreds of buildings, and in each one there are dozens of executives who would benefit from the sort of conversation we just had. But most of them don't have a group of peers to draw on. And this is just one city. There is a huge untapped need."

"Hold on," you are probably thinking, "there are actually endless opportunities for executives to interact." And, on one level, you are right. There are more than a million conferences a year in the US alone, and nearly every vendor in every industry hosts roundtable meetings, webcasts, conferences, or seminars from time to time. Some are substantive, while others are thinly disguised boondoggles or sales pitches. So yes, by one standard, there is a lot of dialogue out there.

Here's the rub: most of these events are well-intentioned, but not very good. And they rarely address the needs of senior executives.

Does this sound familiar? Your firm decides to convene a roundtable meeting for important clients and prospects. An event planner sends out dozens of invitations with little sense of who might attend. Someone invites a speaker, but the objectives are unclear, and the agenda is developed with little input from the participants. One of the firm's "thought leaders" is asked to present or—worse—to facilitate. At best, 20% of the invitees show up, and the meeting fails to generate lasting insights, relationships, or goodwill.

Or how about this scenario? You attend a conference, then sit passively with hundreds of others, watching poorly moderated panels of "experts" pontificate on topics that are only loosely connected, and may not be relevant to your priorities anyway. The keynote speakers might be fun or interesting, particularly if they offer celebrity cachet. But you probably hope the true value of the conference will be revealed during breaks and meals—times when you can find old friends and make new connections.

I get a special kick out of conferences that reserve time for "roundtable" discussions. The conference organizers recognize that attendees want to speak with each other. So, they assemble groups of strangers with no agenda and no clear purpose for the discussion. And while senior executives might present at the conference, few of them stick around to participate in the whole program. Consequently, many of the conference roundtable meetings are stocked with vendors, middle-managers, and industry wannabes looking for jobs. It's not exactly a recipe for success.

Over the course of my professional career, I have found the following to be true. Perhaps you have too.

1. Leadership is more an art than a science, and it is getting more difficult all the time.
2. Beliefs drive our behaviors, and behaviors drive outcomes. So beliefs matter.
3. Leaders are best able to refine their beliefs through conversations with trusted peers.
4. These conversations rarely happen, in part because busy executives have few opportunities to engage with their peers in a meaningful way.
5. Even when a group of peers gets together, the design and nature of their interactions rarely supports an increase in trust over time.

The good news is that well-designed, well-executed executive peer dialogue is possible through private, invitation-only networks. And these networks can be a valuable professional resource for members and sponsors alike. We will explore how.

WHAT DO WE MEAN BY A NETWORK?

Many people have a negative view of networking. We have all attended painful "networking" events, where strangers mingle awkwardly, hoping to make small talk or exchange business cards with a prospective connection. These events are uncomfortable, superficial, and stressful, with perhaps a whiff of desperation. This is not what I am advocating. In many ways, the networks I describe are the exact opposite!

As Eric Sinoway wrote in his excellent book *Howard's Gift* (inspired by legendary Harvard Business School professor Howard Stevenson):

> *"[N]etwork" is a mechanism for providing information and services among a group of people, "relationship" is an emotional connection or involvement between individuals. The difference between those two definitions is significant. So, too, are the practical distinctions between the terms "networking" and "relationship building." Far too many people get the two confused, and I think that's more than just a semantic mix-up ...*
>
> *You should have a conscious, deliberate approach to creating and maintaining this team of catalysts. Why? First, because you want them to be available when you need them. Second, because you don't want to rely on the first people through the door; they may be well-intentioned but lack the particular characteristics, experiences, and perspectives you really need. You should be proactive, even assertive, in identifying your catalysts: go get the people you need!* [1]

That's what we are doing when we convene an executive network: taking a conscious, deliberate approach to creating and maintaining a team of peers who can serve as catalysts.

It may be helpful at this point to illustrate how executive peer networks differ from other convening approaches. Consider the following 2x2 model.

PARTICIPANT EXPERIENCE

		PASSIVE	ACTIVE
PARTICIPANT SCOPE	MULTI-FIRM	**CONFERENCE**	**EXECUTIVE PEER NETWORK**
	SINGLE-FIRM	**PRESENTATION/ BRIEFING**	**LEADERSHIP RETREAT**

This model describes each convening approach along two important dimensions. First, the scope of the participant group. Are participants all from the same organization, or from multiple organizations? Second, the experience for participants, which can range from passive to active.

During corporate presentations, participants passively receive information with their colleagues. Leadership retreats and team off-sites are usually more active, but participation is generally limited to professionals from a single company. Conferences bring together professionals from many different organizations, but the experience is largely passive for most participants. Only executive peer networks deliver active, multi-organization dialogue that engages and inspires participants.

HOW IS THIS BOOK ORGANIZED?

This book is divided into two discrete but interconnected sections. Part 1 offers an overview of several important concepts that should influence the design of any executive peer network. Yes, there is a method to the madness, and I expect you will benefit from these ideas whether or not you take the next step and convene (or join) a network. Part 2 pulls these principles together and offers a design roadmap for executives who want to enhance the impact of their own networks—whether as a participant, convener, or sponsor.

A few other points before you decide whether to read on. First, most people will finish this book in less than an hour. I assume you don't have a lot of time, and don't want to drown you in endless anecdotes, academic theory, or filler. So this is a short book, by design. Second, while it is tempting to dive right into network design and execution, I think you will find it helpful to lay a solid foundation. Finally, you will soon discover that I read a lot, and love to collect and share enlightening or thought-provoking quotes. I included many of my favorites, and trust you will find them to be as insightful and inspiring as I do.

PART I
EIGHT IMPORTANT CONCEPTS

LET'S BEGIN WITH a review of several concepts that provide the basis for effective network and meeting design and execution. You are surely familiar with these terms, but you may not have considered why they matter or how they fit together.

We will examine eight key ideas: community, beliefs, questions, stories, leadership, change, experts, and trust. Together, a deeper appreciation of these ideas will help to illustrate why the right executive peer network can be such a powerful leadership resource—for network members and sponsors alike.

COMMUNITY

Historian Yuval Noah Harari wrote two fascinating books in the last several years, *Sapiens: A Brief History of Humankind*, and its sequel, *Homo Deus: A Brief History of Tomorrow*. He astutely identifies the reason why modern humans have dominated world events since *Homo sapiens* first appeared some 70,000 years ago, while other species have not: "Sapiens can cooperate in extremely flexible ways with countless numbers of strangers. That's why Sapiens rule the world, whereas ants eat our leftovers and chimps are locked up in zoos and research laboratories. ... The ability to create an imagined reality out of words enabled large numbers of strangers to cooperate effectively."[2]

It is natural to speak of collaboration and cooperation in the context of a community. But sociologists frequently disagree about how best to define community. While the term almost always describes people with something in common, some definitions focus on geographic proximity while others believe a community is forged by shared interests or identities without regard to place.

I favor the more expansive definition and believe we are all shaped by our membership in different communities: ethnic, neighborhood, professional, company, hobbies, alma mater, etc. Community norms can strongly influence our behavior, and we expect that membership in those communities will provide certain benefits. After all, "social capital" provides "quite specific benefits that flow from the trust, reciprocity, information, and cooperation associated with social networks."[3]

Much of our work with executives involves building up social capital to enhance the benefits of community membership. But we are also aware of the dark side of communities. As one author wrote, "We band together in 'obvious clubs' that defend competing versions of reality. When you walk into your obvious club, you will find people reading the same books, watching the same news channels, and talking to the same people, all of which tends to reinforce the same version of reality. ... Whatever groups you belong to or most strongly associate with, the dynamics will be similar. Collectively, we create a kind of bubble of belief that reinforces and protects our existing beliefs by denying that alternative beliefs are within the realm of possibility. It's a kind of collective delusion or dream that we co-create in order to maintain a group map that we use to navigate the world. ... It's not possible to have a meaningful dialogue across belief bubbles if people don't feel safe, and safe space requires trust."[4]

Ultimately, executive peer networks are a powerful form of community. As one executive once told us, "your efforts helped form relationships which previously for the most part were rivalries." Another described a network as "a forum to interact with peers who are engaged in the same issues I am, and who face many of the same challenges as I do; it makes me feel less like I am on an island!"

It is precisely because of those dynamics that executive networks can be so valuable. With the right people, addressing the right questions, they can provide many of the benefits common to any strong community: information, cooperation, support, guidance, insight. But in the right hands, they can also provide network members with a new way of thinking about their place in the world, offering tools and perspectives required to navigate leadership challenges—alongside peers who are on the same journey.

BELIEFS

We are bombarded every day with an enormous amount of information. It would be overwhelming to try to take it all in and objectively interpret what it means. So we create mental models—some consciously, many unconsciously. But, of course, our mental models can fail us. In the words of statistician George Box, "All models are wrong, but some are useful."

If you take nothing else away from this book, then please remember this deceptively simple principle:

BELIEFS → BEHAVIORS → OUTCOMES

Your beliefs inevitably impact the way you react to any situation in your life. Different responses then lead to very different outcomes. So, if you want to change any situation, it's not enough to simply change what you do. You must change what you think.

Here is a fun exercise you might try: Take any personal

or professional situation. Maybe you are looking for a new job, or helping your daughter apply to college, or trying to decide on a family vacation. Perhaps you are dealing with an underperforming teammate, deciding between strategic alternatives, or trying to placate an unhappy client. What beliefs are shaping your behaviors? Consider not just your beliefs about the situation, but also beliefs about yourself and others. Why do you believe what you do? And what if you believed something different?

Some beliefs fall into the category of common knowledge—ideas that large numbers of people have collectively agreed to believe (often unconsciously). In fact, most modern social structures depend on shared beliefs in ideas we can't see, feel, or touch (e.g., money, countries, corporations).

But unconscious belief can pose a risk. During his commencement speech at Yale University in 1962, President Kennedy said, "We subject all facts to a prefabricated set of interpretations. We enjoy the comfort of opinion without the discomfort of thought. Mythology distracts us everywhere."

Furthermore, beliefs are not static. They are vulnerable to the steady pace of change. Beliefs that once served you well may no longer hold true.

Consider the computer industry. IBM founder Thomas Watson expressed a belief in 1943 that there was "a world market for maybe five computers." Digital Equipment Corporation founder Ken Olsen had increased this estimate by 1977, though he still believed "There is no reason anyone would want a computer in their home." Bob Metcalfe, co-inventor of the Ethernet, predicted in 1995 that "the Internet will soon go supernova and in 1996 will catastrophically collapse." Former Microsoft CTO Nathan Myhrvold said in 1997 that "Apple is already dead."* And Microsoft founder Bill Gates offered in 2004 that "Two years from now, spam will be solved."

Keep in mind that all these beliefs were offered by experts, people who lived and breathed technology, and had spent countless hours honing beliefs that turned out to be spectacularly wrong. We'll never know how those misguided beliefs shaped their actions and the outcomes for their companies. But it's reasonable to expect that we might be living in a very different world had any of those beliefs been altered just a little—perhaps through better discussions with peers.

QUESTIONS

How do we begin to understand and challenge our beliefs? With questions, of course!

Philosopher Bertrand Russell once advised, "In all affairs it's a healthy thing now and then to hang a question mark on the things you have long taken for granted." Others noted, "The idea behind an opening question is to generate ideas and options, to provoke thought and reveal possibilities, to jumpstart the brain. Good opening questions open doors

---

* To be fair, Myhrvold was not alone. Michael Dell's suggestion for Apple: "I'd shut it down and give the money back to the shareholders."

to new ways of looking at a challenge. The feeling you are striving for is a sense of energy and optimism, where anything is possible. A good opening is a call to adventure."[5]

But questions are a funny thing. Children have no trouble asking questions: When are we going to be there? Why is the sky blue? When are we going to eat? As any parent will attest, children have an endless capacity for questions!

As we grow up, though, too many of us lose the ability to ask good questions. Instead, there is an expectation that adults should start to have all the answers. The curiosity of youth is often replaced by the certainty of adulthood. The child asks, "Why?" and the parent replies, "Because I said so."

But it doesn't have to be this way. Knowledge is power, and good questions can amplify that power. But questioning is hard, and it is a more subtle and complex skill than many realize. Like anything else, asking great questions takes practice.

In my experience, people too often ask closed (yes/no) or leading questions: Do you agree that the President's policies will lead to growth? Will the report be finished by Tuesday?

In contrast, open questions always yield more information, and lead to a richer dialogue: How might the President's policies impact the economy? When do you expect to finish the report? Pay attention to how often you ask closed questions; I suspect you will be surprised.

Whether we're talking about countries, communities, families, or individuals, "we all live in the world our questions create."[6] It is no surprise then that many of the greatest scientists and inventors have pointed to the power of questions. According to Jonas Salk, inventor of the polio vaccine, "What we think of as the moment of discovery is really the discovery of the right question." Einstein once said, "If I had one hour to save the world, I would spend 55 minutes defining the problem and only five minutes finding the solution." And anthropologist Margaret Mead observed that "We are continually faced with great opportunities which are brilliantly disguised as unsolvable problems."

Executive peer networks offer a simple, powerful way for leaders to ask questions of each other, and themselves. And it is rewarding to help leaders reveal previously unconscious beliefs. As a network member once told me, "this forum got me thinking about different ways to approach my job, and I think most others find it helpful in the same way." Another described the value of "insightful questions and discussion leadership. ... I was always able to learn new perspectives and come away from the meetings with new ideas and try them out in real world situations."

STORIES

As any parent knows, if there is one thing a young child loves even more than questions, it's a good story. But what is a story anyway? And are they only for children? Of course not. Some stories are designed merely to entertain. But many have a much deeper purpose.

For centuries, our ancestors used mythology, nursery rhymes, and oral histories to pass along universal wisdom and a framework for ethical decision making. As historian Yuval Noah Harari wrote, "Meaning is created when many people weave together a common network of stories. ... Humans think they make history, but history actually revolves around the web of stories."[7]

There are many classic narrative structures. Consider Joseph Campbell's "The Hero's Journey" narrative pattern, for example. Powerful stories typically involve a protagonist overcoming an obstacle, such as man, nature, society, or oneself.

Storytelling is an increasingly important business skill. As Rolf Jensen from the Copenhagen Institute for Future Studies said, "We are in the twilight of a society based on data. As information and intelligence become the domain of computers, society will place new value on the one human ability that cannot be automated: emotion. Imagination, myth, ritual—the language of emotion—will affect everything from our purchasing decisions to how well we work with others. Companies will thrive on the basis of their stories and myths. Companies will need to understand that their products are less important than their stories."[8]

During network meetings, I often ask members to share personal anecdotes that illustrate a point. Sometimes it is a success story. Sometimes it is a story about failure or a missed opportunity. Like peeling an onion, even the simplest story can take on new life when the central facts are subject to questions like who, what, where, when, why, and how. Stories provide an emotional anchor for any discussion. And the story behind the story is often more fascinating than the story itself.

LEADERSHIP

Leadership is not for the faint of heart. According to a 2014 report by the Center for Creative Leadership, "The life of a modern-day leader clearly is not easy. Inside their organizations, they need to lead and motivate a diversified group of people, work across organizational boundaries, improve efficiency, and achieve growth. Externally, they face a complex and globalized environment; they have to manage the requirements of government, keep up with competitors, and meet the expectations of other stakeholders. And within this global environment, there are many cultural considerations leaders must face to be effective. They must work across cultural boundaries and alongside others who, at times, are very different from them and have different ways of getting work completed. These are difficult challenges, and many leaders feel ill-prepared to tackle them."[9]

Since this book posits that leaders benefit from more—and better—engagement with peers, let me offer a few other thoughts about leadership.

The first is that leadership is a noun; leading is a verb. As Simon Sinek said, "there are leaders and there are those who lead."[10] I love that distinction. Leadership is more than a title. Titles may provide a platform, but the work of leadership is active, the pursuit of opportunity.

Second, the scope of a leader's job continues to expand with no end in sight. At the same time, many leaders feel like they have less and less control. This is the product, at least in part, of increasingly interconnected global trade, economic, and information systems. Few leaders can understand the complex system well enough to predict outcomes, and this can be deeply unsettling. Leaders are presented with so many alternatives, and yet historical data may be of little value trying to anticipate the best course of action.

A third and final point about leadership. When I worked at Harvard Business School, we were frequently asked about the difference between leaders and managers. We usually described it this way: the manager figures out the best way to hack a path through the jungle, while the leader decides what jungle to go through.

But that distinction now seems inadequate. Should we even go through the jungle? What if we could fly over the trees? Or tunnel under them? The irony is that as leaders' schedules get more crowded, they need even more time for reflection and creative problem solving. They need to gain new perspective on their challenges and new insights into possible-solutions—the type of perspective that sometimes only peers can offer.

CHANGE

Many people believe Charles Darwin wrote about the survival of the fittest. But that phrase was actually coined by Herbert

Spencer. What Darwin wrote in *On The Origin of the Species* was: "It is not the strongest of the species that survives, nor the most intelligent, but the ones most responsive to change."

In many ways, leadership is about navigating change. And executive peer networks often form when leaders recognize that their own perspective is inadequate in the face of regulatory, technological, or market changes.

Klaus Schwab of the World Economic Forum writes in his thought-provoking book, *The Fourth Industrial Revolution*, about

> *an underlying theme in my conversations with global CEOs and senior business executives; namely, that the deluge of information available today, the velocity of disruption and the acceleration of innovation are hard to comprehend or anticipate. They constitute a source of constant surprise. In such a context, it is a leader's ability to continually learn, adapt and challenge his or her own conceptual and operating models of success that will distinguish the next generation of successful business leaders.[11]*

I had a fascinating conversation several years ago with a seasoned business executive and scholar who observed that change has three dimensions:

1. *Technical,* including commercial, scientific, financial, regulatory, legal considerations. This is usually straight-forward to understand.

2. *Political,* which can be tricky given the important role of power, motivations, interests, and influence in shaping change.
3. *Cultural,* which is often the hardest to navigate. The leader needs to factor in issues of identity, beliefs, memory, history, and norms within and across groups.

The vexing reality is that change is both inevitable and unpredictable. Indeed, the future is getting harder to predict with any confidence. This has many consequences. For example, according to historian Yuval Noah Harari, "Since we do not know how the job market would look in 2030 or 2040, already today we have no idea what to teach our kids. Most of what they currently learn at school will probably be irrelevant by the time they are forty."[12]

Savvy executives know that their own experience represents only a small part of the whole picture. And while each leader's context is different, they often share common objectives. To better navigate a world of accelerating change and uncertainty, executives will need to draw on trusted relationships with peers who offer timely insight, guidance, and support.

EXPERTS

We value expertise, and for good reason. After all, only experts could put a man on the moon, or turn crude oil into a plastic toy. In these situations, experts have mastered the well-understood relationship between actions and outcomes.

But expertise can be dangerous too. As author Joshua Lehrer pointed out,

> *Knowledge can be a subtle curse. When we learn about the world, we also learn all the reasons why the world cannot be changed. We get used to our failures and imperfections. We become numb to the possibilities of something new. In fact, the only way to remain creative over time—to not be undone by our expertise—is to experiment with ignorance, to stare at things we don't fully understand.*[13]

Famed architect Frank Lloyd Wright, clearly an expert himself, once described an expert as someone who has "stopped thinking because he 'knows.'" Another expert, legendary basketball coach John Wooden, once said, "It's what you learn after you know everything that counts."

There is value in inviting thoughtful, open-minded people to look at a problem, even if they lack specific domain expertise. A new perspective can completely change the way we see a situation and our self-interest with respect to it. As economist John Maynard Keynes observed, "The difficulty lies not so much in developing new ideas as in escaping from old ones."

Yet, too many experts are blinded by hubris. As Bill Gates once asserted, "success is a lousy teacher. It seduces smart people into thinking they can't lose." And Mark Twain famously stated: "It *ain't* what you don't know that gets you into trouble. It's what you know for sure that *just ain't* so."

Although the members of an executive peer network are typically experts in their industry or role, many lack broad exposure to other disciplines. Consequently, there is much value in helping these leaders to expand their horizon. As an executive once told me, "the diversity of your work makes you more valuable. You have a very unique perspective and can better 'connect the dots' in new ways. And corporate innovation is really combining existing things in new ways for new purposes."

TRUST

We know intuitively that trust is a fundamental quality for any leader. After all, "[t]rust is the essential glue that binds together the complex networks of participants involved in the creation of economic value (customers, business partners, and other stakeholders)."[14]

But what exactly is trust? What contributes to trust? And is trust given or earned? We know that relationships and trust are dynamic. They either improve and evolve, or they wither on the vine.

I'm not inclined to dedicate much space here to the factors that enhance or destroy trust. Countless articles, and indeed entire books, have been written on the topic. They often list qualities such as clarity, compassion, character, contribution, competency, connection, commitment, and consistency. Author and speaker Keith Ferrazzi says the "Four Mind-Sets" for relationships are candor, vulnerability, accountability, and generosity.[15] And a popular consulting equation holds that trustworthiness = (credibility + reliability + intimacy)/self-orientation.[16]

I tend to view authenticity as a key to trust. Say what you mean, and mean what you say, without any pretense or hidden agenda. "Fake it 'til you make it" fools nobody.

Instead of debating specific words and concepts, let's just agree that trust is an input to—and an output of—effective dialogue: "Dialogue involves a relationship built on trusting, caring questions; when practiced well and often, dialogue builds trust, as people see that their questions and observations are appreciated. Central to the concept of dialogue is the idea that through the interaction, people acknowledge the wholeness of others—not just their utility. The focus is on acquiring greater understanding and attaining shared meaning."[17]

Klaus Schwab argued that, "Boundaries between sectors and professions are artificial and are proving to be increasingly counterproductive. More than ever, it is essential to dissolve these barriers by engaging the power of networks to forge effective partnerships. ... In a world where nothing is constant anymore, trust becomes one of the most valuable attributes."[18]

The lesson here is clear. Trust is a critical ingredient in the design and delivery of any effective executive peer network. Without trust, there is little to hold a group together.

I said there was a method to the madness. Let's talk about what to do next.

PART 2
CREATING EXECUTIVE NETWORKS

I N THE FIRST part of this book, I laid out the following argument:

1. Leadership is more an art than a science, and it is getting more difficult all the time.
2. Beliefs drive behaviors, and behaviors drive outcomes.
3. Leaders are best able to refine their beliefs through conversations with trusted peers.
4. These relationships rarely happen, in part because busy executives have few opportunities to engage with their peers in a meaningful way.
5. Even when a group of peers gets together, the design and nature of their interactions rarely supports an increase in trust over time.

In Part 2, we will focus on some of the principles my colleagues and I have found helpful in building and sustaining executive peer networks whose value increases over time. This usually requires two phases: initial network design, and ongoing network execution. We'll look at each, but with a greater focus on network design.

WHAT ARE THE CHARACTERISTICS OF GREAT EXECUTIVE PEER NETWORKS?

As venture capitalist and entrepreneur Rich Stromback observed, "Nobody wants to have a 'networking conversation,' especially those who are at the highest levels of business and politics. They are hungry for real conversations and real relationships. It just has to be authentic, genuine and sincere."[19]

Entrepreneur and writer Tim Askew agrees: "Much of networking just seems to smack of manipulation and insincerity. When I hear people talking about networking, the verbiage always seems undergirded with an assumption of venality and calculation. And that includes those whose networking philosophy is 'you get by giving.' Even that philosophy of networking has the root assumption of giving as ultimately a manipulation to get what you want, rather than real generosity of spirit. ... My own general feeling is that most networking is a distracting, energy vitiating waste of time."[20]

However, Askew continues:

There is only one form of networking that makes sense to me, and that is networking with peers—networking with fellow CEOs, owners, seekers, and entrepreneurs—hopefully through relaxed, open-ended personal conversations that allow development of relationships in a general atmosphere of collegiality. … For me, frenetic, frequent, voluminous communication doesn't equate to thoughtful and effective communication. What I am looking for is real connection. Isn't everyone? Quantity of conversation cannot substitute for quality of conversation. [21]

Let's face it: executives are invited to attend seminars, presentations, receptions, and roundtable meetings all the time. But many executives are overwhelmed by the demands on their time. To cut through the noise, a network leader must design and deliver a truly distinctive experience. It must be something members look forward to and feel invested in. Something they will travel for, and adapt their schedule around. Something they belong to, not something they attend.

This, in a nutshell, is what we are talking about. Quality, thoughtful, ongoing conversation with peers in an atmosphere of collegiality. A trust-based "network" rather than transactional "networking." But where to find one?

NOT ALL NETWORKS ARE ALIKE

Have you ever done a Google search to look for executive peer networks? I have, and it can be eye opening. With minimal effort, you will uncover dozens (or even hundreds) of "executive communities." And new groups are springing up all the time.

Many are simply online contact databases, designed to facilitate job searches or sales leads. Some are membership organizations that host breakfasts, cocktail parties, educational events, and community service projects for a cohort (e.g., young professionals, corporate board members) in a local community. There are a few that offer in-person meetings in small groups, though members rarely play a meaningful role in shaping the meeting agenda.

Despite the transactional nature of members' interactions, many of these organizations laud the benefits members will derive from the group. For example, they say things like:

- "[members] have the ability to establish more robust connections than in other executive organizations."
- "we offer events with capped attendance so that you have a better opportunity for personal interaction to truly network and develop friendships."
- "[the group] is about developing leads ... you will walk away with more leads."
- "Our bond of friendship and trust makes the sharing of active searches possible."

I don't believe it. The design of most of these "networks" will never yield the promised results. This is not to say that they are without merit, though.

Let's acknowledge that online "communities" can be helpful, in some cases. As a Harvard Business School alumnus, I have access to a searchable database of more than 80,000 fellow alumni. Many of those people respect our shared affiliation and will respond to a cold email inquiry from a fellow alumnus. I have been on both the sending and receiving ends of that equation. But access to a mailing list does little to generate the sort of quality, thoughtful discussion leaders need.

Few executive communities are alike, and their differences can often be revealed through the following questions:

- Who organizes the group and how is it funded?
- What benefits do members and/or sponsors derive from their investment?
- How often do members meet, and what is the format of the meetings?
- How large is the group?
- What are the membership criteria and how are members selected?
- Who sets the meeting agendas, who leads the conversations, and how do members participate?
- How engaged do members feel in the group?
- What are members' objectives in joining the group (regardless of whether they pay to belong)?
- How much time are members expected to commit to the group?

WHY THE FOCUS ON ROUNDTABLE MEETINGS?

You have surely experienced the limitations of many convening formats, including conferences, networking events, and online communities. However, there is one format that has the *potential* to foster consistently great discussion: roundtables. This format typically involves 6 to 16 people—as many as fit comfortably around a large table. Roundtables offer a balance between breadth and intimacy, in a setting that allows participants to talk *with* each other, not *at* each other. With the right people, the right setting, the right agenda, and the right facilitator, a roundtable meeting can be magical.

Sadly, too many roundtable meetings fall short of that aspirational outcome. After all, it is not difficult to throw together a mediocre, one-off roundtable meeting. Often, a senior person agrees to organize the event but then fails to invest the time or resources to do it right. The event goes forward, but the content and experience are unremarkable. Most successful executives will only attend such an event if they have nothing better to do. And they always have something better to do.

Having led executive-level roundtable meetings for more than 13 years, I am convinced that the quality of any meeting is determined long before the group comes together. It is important to: invite the right people; listen carefully to their challenges and expectations; design an agenda that balances disparate priorities; and allow participants to reflect on key issues in advance. The meeting leader should respect the topic's natural ebb and flow, guiding the discussion with a light touch. Any conversation worth having is worth documenting, and the leader should distribute a concise summary soon after the meeting. These activities all require skill, experience, and commitment, but the effort often yields substantial value.

CASE STUDY: INNOVATORS COUNCIL

To illustrate my point, let's consider an industry-specific meeting I attended several years ago. I didn't know much about the industry, but thought it might be a good way to meet some new people and learn a thing or two along the way. The meeting was convened by a professional who organized similar events around the country. And it was hosted by a prominent firm in their conference facility.

About 25 people showed up, representing a variety of roles: customers, vendors, consultants, and other subject matter experts. Following introductions, we watched a few promotional videos and presentations, designed solely to credentialize the convener. We then split into breakout groups. Each group was asked to "brainstorm" how particular innovations might be adapted to various customer segments, by arranging Post-it notes on a wall. Breakout teams then reported their insights back to the whole group. The meeting facilitator summarized the conversation, and asked the group how they would like to proceed; should we reconvene to brainstorm again or dig deeper into one or more ideas that had been raised?

I received an email a few days after the event with a bold title: "Boston Innovators Workshop A Success." The email further observed that "Participants overwhelmingly voted to continue the conversation, so we will be back in Boston on December 3. New participants are welcome, and will not be disadvantaged by not attending the first workshop."

Did participants really vote overwhelmingly to continue the conversation? That was not my sense at all. Rather, people nodded politely when the facilitator proposed another meeting. I had no interest in coming back, and I would be willing to bet most others felt the same. Despite spending three hours together, I made no lasting relationships and didn't even have access to a list of my fellow attendees.

I recently located a web page with a short summary of the follow-up meeting. As far as I can tell, that meeting simply featured presentations by vendors offering collaboration solutions. The worst thing: I was in a picture on the web page that contained a synopsis of this second meeting (i.e., the one I didn't attend). Talk about violating my trust!

So, what went wrong? In short, there were at least five major flaws in both the design and execution of this "council."

1. There was no agenda. We all showed up without knowing who else would be there, or how we would be spending our time.
2. The facilitator never asked why participants were there, or what they hoped to discuss and achieve.
3. The participants were not peers. It was a strange

hodge-podge of people who had been invited by different people for different reasons. Consequently, our expertise and interest in the topics varied widely.

4. The meeting "close" felt forced. Why would we want to brainstorm or go deeper? After all, we had no shared objective, and there was no need for us to reach consensus.

5. The meeting featured style over substance. The videos and PowerPoint decks were long on razzle-dazzle and short on depth. The follow-up email was promotional and self-congratulatory.

Why does this experience continue to stand out after many years? In short, because it so clearly confirmed the merits of an alternate approach.

NETWORK DESIGN

At their core, networks are a tactic. An effective network should help a diverse group of stakeholders to realize their strategic objectives. This includes network members, sponsors, and even the network leader. But this is not a simple feat. Sponsors and members rarely have the same objectives. In fact, their objectives may diverge in important ways. And even within a group of network members, there is rarely uniformity in beliefs, interests, or circumstances. A network that fails to recognize its stakeholders' divergent objectives may survive for a while, but will eventually collapse under its own weight.

It is important to choose from various design alternatives that will provide a strong network foundation. This step applies whether the network is initiated by members, by third-party sponsors, or by an experienced network leadership firm.

It is usually helpful to ask prospective members and sponsors open-ended questions early in the network design process. Common questions include:

- What challenges and opportunities are you facing?
- How might a network help you to address them?
- What alternatives would satisfy those same needs if a network didn't exist?
- What membership criteria would lead to the best conversations?
- How might we determine the membership list?
- What value could the network offer to participants?
- What are the advantages and disadvantages of seeking network sponsors?
- Which sponsors would be most suitable?
- When and where should we hold meetings?
- What format(s) might be most effective?
- How much time and money are you willing to spend?
- Who should lead the meeting?

NETWORK LEADER CHOICE

One of the first and most important decisions is the choice of network leader. This person (or people, in the case of co-leaders) will be responsible for design and execution decisions, including choices about network governance (e.g., new members, network practices, decision authority).

For informal or self-organized groups, the network leader is often the person who first proposed the idea of getting together. Meeting leadership responsibility may rotate, but it is likely that the original advocate will play an outsized role in the direction of the group, as *primus inter pares*.

When vendors decide to convene an executive roundtable meeting, the leader is typically a senior partner or client-facing professional with enough market credibility to invite important clients and prospects. This could be a practice leader, functional leader, service line leader, or business unit leader. Although many of the tactical details are delegated to subordinates (including event planners and administrative staff), this network leader has primary responsibility for delivering a successful program.

Unlike self-organized or vendor-led networks, network leaders from third-party firms often design and deliver executive network programs for a living. An independent meeting facilitator can identify and move the group into areas that would be more challenging for a participant or chair with a direct stake in the outcome of the conversation. And even though they may lack the immediate market credibility that comes with domain expertise, third-party network leaders typically offer battle-tested experience, a creative generalist mindset, and skills that are well suited to the task at hand.

An effective network leader should always demonstrate

the 7 Cs. He or she should be: creative, connected, candid, courageous, collaborative, confident, and credible. In addition, the leader should possess the following skills and attributes:

- Synthesis: organizing common themes, recognizing patterns
- Interviewing and listening
- Meeting facilitation: small groups, large groups
- Agenda design: narrative, flow, pace
- Authenticity and the ability to build trusting relationships
- Well-developed communication skills: verbal, written
- Balance of intuition and analysis: what questions flow from the facts?
- Vision for the group over time

MEMBERSHIP CRITERIA

Executive peer networks are made up of people, so it should be no surprise that membership criteria drive many of the other network design decisions. Clear criteria help the network leader and/or sponsors to determine who might be invited to join the network, and who shouldn't be.

Networks are often launched in response to shifts in an executive role or industry (e.g., regulatory, demographic, technological). As a starting point, it can be helpful to fill in the following sentence:

[This group of people] should meet more often to discuss [these topics] because of [these changes that are impacting them].

There are several membership criteria that might be applied, but in my experience the six most common are:

- Industry
- Role/title (including tenure in the job)
- Organization characteristics (e.g., size, complexity, public/private)
- Geography (e.g., local, regional, national, global)
- Demographic factors (e.g., gender, race, nationality, age)
- Affiliation with sponsors (e.g., clients, prospects)

The art of network design is to mix and match these criteria so that the group is large and diverse enough without being overwhelming. For example, a network focused only on "technology executives" would never fly; there is too little specificity. However, a network of technology company CFOs from US-based public companies with market capitalization over $10 billion might yield a reasonable number of candidates. With a narrower group of candidates typically comes a tighter set of common challenges, and a richer shared set of discussion topics.

Setting membership criteria is often an iterative effort. For example, how might the network change if we reduced the market cap threshold to $5 billion or raised it to $20 billion. What if we included Canadian companies? European companies? What if we limited the group to companies in the Bay Area? What if we only included CFOs who had been in their jobs for more than three years, or focused only on new CFOs (i.e., less than a year). And does "technology" include biotechnology, or are we more focused on information technology? Each tweak changes the pool of qualified members and the character of the group.

MEETINGS: FREQUENCY, TIMING, FORMAT, LOCATION

It's not enough to just decide who should be invited to join a peer network. Members must also agree on the nature of their interactions. And these decisions are connected. For example, a network of executives in a single city might decide to meet for breakfast monthly, but this format and frequency would be impractical for a network of senior executives who live all over the United States.

I lean toward three meetings a year for most networks. Monthly or quarterly usually feels too frequent, particularly given that several blocks of time rarely work (e.g., summer, year-end). And, with a semi-annual pace, members who miss a meeting go a whole year between formal touchpoints with the group. It's hard for network members to feel connected to peers they see infrequently. In my experience, three times a year strikes the right balance—with regular meetings so the group can develop a cadence, but spaced out enough to avoid meeting fatigue.

There is no "right" meeting format either. Some groups convene for dinner, then meet all or part of the next day. The informal connections over dinner may foster a more collegial conversation in the morning. However, I usually prefer a 3–4-hour roundtable meeting starting mid-afternoon, followed by a group dinner. This allows participants to travel the same day as the meeting and/or leave on the last flight out. And a 3–4-hour meeting allows the group to cover a substantive agenda without rushing. Longer meetings risk losing focus or defaulting to more passive formats (e.g., presentations). I also find that a casual dinner is a nice way to end the meeting, as members unwind together after a day of structured conversation. Members inevitably start to share personal details—family, vacations, career path—and these personal bonds enhance trust over time.

The choice of meeting location will, of course, be determined by members' homes and the "center of gravity" for the industry or role, if one exists. It is usually helpful to test one or two likely meeting venues as the network is being designed so that members can factor travel into their decision to join the network.

Before we move on, I would like to make a point about dialing into network meetings. In short, don't allow it! Nothing kills the vibe of a meeting more than a group of people staring at a Polycom on the table or squirming awkwardly as telephone participants try to inject themselves into the conversation without sensing the body language in the room. Although those on the phone might appreciate the ability to listen in, the benefits are one-sided, and the practice does nothing to build trust. Of course, competing priorities will inevitably keep some members from attending every meeting. But it's far better to debrief non-attendees after the fact. Trust me on this. It's not even close.

CONTENT AGENDA

It is helpful to start thinking during the design phase about a range of topics that will provide value to members and/or sponsors. Topics typically fall into three categories:

- External events, which may include regulatory, demographic, or technical developments. Sometimes, these topics are best addressed with the help of experts, so that network members can explore why and how external events matter.
- Internal practices, which vary widely by role, industry, and geography. We resist the term "best practices," though some practices will clearly be more effective than others.
- Personal and professional challenges. These can be particularly helpful since there is often little relevant literature available. Executives often welcome opportunities to speak candidly with peers about career issues, professional challenges (e.g., staying motivated, time management), and personal concerns (e.g., how to avoid raising spoiled kids).

SPONSORSHIP

The choice of sponsors is critical to the success of a network. Network sponsors typically defray many of the costs of running the network, including the meeting leader's professional fees and expenses, meeting space, audiovisual, food/beverage, printing/mailing, and ground transportation. While financial support is a precondition of sponsorship, it is not enough. Anyone can write a check, and the best sponsors often bring valuable insights, relationships, and perspectives to the network.

Sponsors will naturally expect to derive commercial benefits from the conversation. However, it is both unrealistic and unhelpful to measure the short-term value of network sponsorship. Over the long term, sponsors will often win new work; enhance their ability to defend, retain, or expand existing client relationships; and gain proprietary market insights. Sponsors may also capture the value associated with proprietary network content and may leverage the relationships, insights, or brand value of the network to develop talent, improve internal processes, and influence important stakeholders.

For many sponsors, there is also brand value in demonstrating support for an important constituency. As marketing expert Bernadette Jiwa wrote, the key question for any company is: "How can you become more relevant and significant to the people you want to serve? How can your business be about making them live as a better version of themselves? What difference does your product make to them?"[22]

CONFIDENTIALITY PRINCIPLES

It is helpful to adopt unambiguous confidentiality principles. Nothing will chill discussion and undermine a network faster than a nagging concern that comments made during network meetings (or pre-meeting calls with the network leader) will come back later to bite the speaker.

We typically use a modified version of the Chatham House Rule (CHR). This rule is named after the headquarters of the UK Royal Institute of International Affairs, based at Chatham House, London, where the rule originated in 1927 and was refined in 2002. The rule states:

> *When a meeting, or part thereof, is held under the Chatham House Rule, participants are free to use the information received, but neither the identity nor the affiliation of the speaker(s), nor that of any other participant, may be revealed.*

According to the Chatham House website, the CHR "allows people to speak as individuals, and to express views that may not be those of their organizations, and therefore it encourages free discussion. People usually feel more relaxed if they don't have to worry about their reputation or the implications if they are publicly quoted."[23]

The CHR prescribes that "the list of attendees should not

be circulated beyond those participating in the meeting." However, we often modify the rule slightly and allow participants' names to be shared publicly. Still, any content coming out of the meeting must be carefully sanitized, to ensure that quotes or other references are not traceable back to the speaker (e.g., eliminating references to a speaker's industry, role, gender).

NETWORK LAUNCH AND NETWORK LIFE

After the network has been designed, it is time to recruit members and launch the network. The network leader typically works with sponsors to generate a comprehensive list of executives who fit the membership criteria. Together, they then prioritize the list and identify four or five "anchor tenants" whose early commitment will legitimize the network and attract others to participate. These anchor tenants are often well-known to either the sponsor or network leader.

Once the network is recruited, it's time to schedule the first meeting. Preparation here is critical. The network leader should speak with each member before the meeting to understand their needs and shape the agenda around shared priorities. These conversations are more than just a tactic to generate agenda topics. In fact, the discussions can be a significant source of value on their own. As a network member once told us, "I've enjoyed our many conversations, perhaps just as much as the events themselves. I think you figured out how to tap into the differences of this job from others, indulging perhaps our tendency for some amount of drama."

We won't get too much into meeting execution, as my goal in this book is to provide you with a high-level network design framework, not a checklist of action steps once the network is up and running. But of course, a successful meeting requires event planning, administrative support (both on-site and off-site), content development and distribution, and a meeting leadership plan. The meeting should flow, with periods of divergence and convergence, and a set of open-ended questions that foster a cohesive discussion narrative. And the network leader should prepare a summary of each meeting to share with the group afterwards (including non-attending members).

Over time, network meetings will become deeper and more nuanced, as members move from discussions of low-hanging fruit and start tapping rich veins of angst or insight. And the meeting leader should explore innovative ways to keep the network fresh, such as proposing offbeat topics, mixing up the format, or planning an off-site meeting.

Since networks are a tactic, it is helpful to periodically revisit the assumptions that informed the initial network design. Members or sponsors may find that their needs have changed, and it is useful to consider ways to modify the network design—with new members, new sponsors, new discussion topics, and new meeting formats. This network evolution is both healthy and inevitable.

FINAL THOUGHTS

WE ARE LIVING in exciting, challenging, scary times. The nature of work itself is in flux. There is much opportunity, but also much risk and uncertainty.

Business is not just business anymore. Business is personal. And executives need more than ever to nurture their relationships and professional networks. In a transactional world, they need to belong.

I've seen the power of executive peer networks firsthand. And I envision a future in which these networks are as integral to professional success as a personal computer or a smartphone.

In my vision, every executive has two lists. First, a list of 20 peers he or she would most like to spend time with on a regular basis. Some of these may be competitors; that's ok. There are almost always important, non-competitive issues to explore. Second, a list of 20 clients or prospects he or she would like to know better, in a non-transactional setting. As a network sponsor, the executive can bring these people together, to listen and learn as they discuss priorities and challenges with each other.

I trust this short book has given you much to think about, and hope we have an opportunity to discuss these ideas in person one day.

ACKNOWLEDGMENTS

IT HAS BEEN a joy to write this book, in part because so many people have helped to make it better along the way.

I first started thinking seriously about executive peer networks when I joined Tapestry Networks in 2004. Over the next nine years, I had the pleasure of collaborating with many outstanding colleagues, sponsors, and network members. Our time together fueled my passion for this work and laid the groundwork for many of the ideas in this book. Thanks to George Goldsmith, Mark Bonchek, and the late Cory Lefebvre for founding Tapestry and for inviting me to join in the early days.

In 2013, I left Tapestry to launch SkyBridge Associates with the help of a talented young colleague, Kristen Alpaugh, and the counsel of a mentor, Tom Woodard. Collectively, we spent hundreds of hours refining the principles that lead to distinctive executive peer networks. Brooke Lindblad has been a superb addition to the SkyBridge family, and Perry Lane recently joined the team as a trusted advisor and sounding board—both on the publication of this book and on SkyBridge strategy more generally.

Many friends, clients, and colleagues have taken the time to offer their feedback and suggestions on various drafts of this book. Special thanks to George Anderson, Sarah Green Carmichael, George Watts, Mary Carol Mazza, and Mark Tresnowski. I have valued your support and input more than you know.

Finally, the biggest thanks go to my family. To my parents, who instilled in me a curiosity and love of learning that grows stronger by the day. To my brother and sister, for our shared adventures and my first peer group. To my amazing kids, Hailey, Evan, and Casey, who are all fun, interesting, passionate, and kind. They make every day brighter. And I owe a debt I can never repay to my wife, Maribeth, who has supported and encouraged my every dream. She is my biggest fan, and none of this would be possible without her.

ADDITIONAL RESOURCES

I HAVE INCLUDED A reference list of books, articles, and videos that have inspired my thinking over the last several years. You may find some of these to be useful as well.

Asacker, Tom. *The Business of Belief: How the World's Best Marketers, Designers, Salespeople, Coaches, Fundraisers, Educators, Entrepreneurs and Other Leaders Get Us to Believe.* CreateSpace, 2013.

Beinhocker, Eric D. *The Origin of Wealth: Evolution, Complexity, and the Radical Remaking of Economics.* Harvard Business School, 2007.

Bojer, Marianne Mille. *Mapping Dialogue: Essential Tools for Social Change.* Taos Institute Publications, 2008.

Brabandere, Luc de, and Alan Iny. *Thinking in New Boxes: A New Paradigm for Business Creativity.* Random House, 2013.

Ertel, C., & Solomon, L. K. *Moments of impact: How to design strategic conversations that accelerate change.* Simon & Schuster, 2014.

Fisher, Roger, William Ury, and Bruce Patton. *Getting to Yes: Negotiating Agreement Without Giving In.* Penguin, 2011.

Glaser, Judith E. *Conversational Intelligence: How Great Leaders Build Trust & Get Extraordinary Results.* Routledge, 2016.

Godin, Seth. *Graceful: Making a Difference in a World That Needs You.* Do You Zoom Inc., 2010.

Gray, Dave. *Liminal Thinking: Create the Change You Want by Changing the Way You Think.* Rosenfeld Media, 2016.

Gray, David, and Thomas Vander Wal. *The Connected Company.* O'Reilly Media, 2012.

Gray, David, Sunni Brown, and James Macanufo. *Gamestorming: A Playbook for Innovators, Rulebreakers, and Changemakers.* O'Reilly Media, 2010.

Halpin, Katharine. *Alignment for Success: Bringing Out the Best in Yourself, Your Teams, and Your Company.* Vollor Guenther, 2014.

Harari, Yuval Noah. *Homo Deus: A Brief History of Tomorrow.* HarperCollins, 2017.

Harari, Yuval Noah. *Sapiens: A Brief History of Humankind.* Harper, 2015.

Heath, Chip, and Dan Heath. *Made to Stick: Why Some Ideas Survive and Others Die.* Random House, 2007.

Heath, Chip, and Dan Heath. *Switch: How to Change Things When Change Is Hard.* Broadway Books, 2010.

Ibarra, Herminia, and Kent Lineback. "What's Your Story?" *Harvard Business Review,* January 2005.

Jiwa, Bernadette. *Difference: The one-page method for reimagining your business and reinventing your marketing.* CreateSpace, 2014.

Jiwa, Bernadette. *Meaningful: The Story of Ideas That Fly.* Perceptive Press, 2015.

Jiwa, Bernadette. *Marketing: A Love Story: How to Matter to Your Customers.* CreateSpace, 2014.

Johnson, Mark W. *Seizing the White Space: Business Model Innovation for Growth and Renewal.* Harvard Business School Press, 2010.

Kahane, Adam. *Solving Tough Problems: An Open Way of Talking, Listening, and Creating New Realities.* Berrett-Koehler, 2004.

Kao, John. *Clearing the Mind for Creativity.* FTPress, 2010.

Kaplan, Saul. *The Business Model Innovation Factory: How to Stay Relevant When the World Is Changing.* Wiley, 2012.

Kaputa, Catherine. *You Are a Brand!: In Person and Online, How Smart People Brand Themselves for Business Success.* Nicholas Brealey, 2012.

Kuhlman, David C. *Leading Firms: How Great Professional Service Firms Succeed and How Your Firm Can Too.* SelectBooks, 2013.

LeFever, Lee. *The Art of Explanation: Making your Ideas, Products, and Services Easier to Understand.* Wiley, 2012.

Lehrer, Jonah. *Imagine: How Creativity Works.* Houghton Mifflin, 2012.

Love, Howard. *The Start-Up J Curve: The Six Steps to Entrepreneurial Success.* Greenleaf Book Group Press, 2016.

Lucas, Peter and Joe Ballay, Mickey McManus. *Trillions: Thriving in the Emerging Information Ecology.* Wiley, 2012.

Maister, David H., Charles H. Green, and Robert M. Galford. *The Trusted Advisor.* Touchstone, 2001.

Marquardt, Michael J. *Leading with Questions: How Leaders Find the Right Solutions by Knowing What to Ask.* Jossey-Bass, 2014.

Martin, Roger L. *The Opposable Mind: Winning Through Integrative Thinking.* Harvard Business School Press, 2009.

McGoff, Chris. *The Primes: How Any Group Can Solve Any Problem.* Wiley, 2012.

Meadows, Martin. *How to Think Bigger: Aim Higher, Get More Motivated, and Accomplish Big Things.* Meadows, 2015.

Meyer, Christopher, and Julia Kirby. *Standing on the Sun: How the Explosion of Capitalism Abroad Will Change Business Everywhere.* Harvard Business School Press, 2012.

Patel, Mona. *Reframe: Shift the Way You Work, Innovate, and Think.* Lioncrest, 2015.

Pink, Daniel H. *Drive: The Surprising Truth About What Motivates Us.* Riverhead Books, 2011.

Port, Michael. *Book Yourself Solid: The Fastest, Easiest, and Most Reliable System for Getting More Clients Than You Can Handle Even If You Hate Marketing and Selling.* Wiley, 2011.

Raynor, Michael E. *The Strategy Paradox: Why committing to success leads to failure (and what to do about it).* Crown Business, 2007.

Roberts, Laura M., Gretchen Spreitzer, Jane Dutton, Robert Quinn, Emily Heaphy, and Brianna Barker. "How to Play to Your Strengths." *Harvard Business Review,* January 2005.

Roth, Bernard. *The Achievement Habit: Stop Wishing, Start Doing, and Take Command of Your Life.* HarperBusiness, 2015.

Rumelt, Richard P. *Good Strategy, Bad Strategy: The Difference and Why It Matters.* Crown Business, 2011.

Schein, Edgar H. *Humble Inquiry: The Gentle Art of Asking Instead of Telling.* Berrett-Koehler, 2013.

Schwab, Klaus. *The Fourth Industrial Revolution.* Crown Business, 2017.

Schwarz, Roger M. *The Skilled Facilitator: Practical Wisdom for Developing Effective Groups.* Jossey-Bass, 2001.

Scott, S.J. *S.M.A.R.T. Goals Made Simple: 10 Steps to Master Your Personal and Career Goals.* Oldtown, 2014.

Sedniev, Andrii. *The Business Idea Factory: A World-Class System for Creating Successful Business Ideas,* CreateSpace, 2013.

Sibbet, David. *Visual Meetings: How Graphics, Sticky Notes, & Idea Mapping Can Transform Group Productivity.* John Wiley & Sons, 2010.

Sinoway, Eric. *Howard's Gift: Uncommon Wisdom to Inspire Your Life's Work.* Griffin, 2013.

Smith, Paul. *Lead with a Story: A Guide to Crafting Business Narratives That Captivate, Convince, and Inspire.* AMACOM, 2012.

Snowden, Dave. "How to organise a Children's Party." *YouTube.* October 2009.

Snowden, David J., and Mary E. Boone. "A Leader's Framework for Decision Making." *Harvard Business Review,* November 2007.

Sobel, Andrew, and Jerold Panas. *Power Questions: Build Relationships, Win New Business, and Influence Others.* Wiley, 2012.

Sullivan, Chatham. *The Clarity Principle: How Great Leaders Make the Most Important Decision in Business (and What Happens When They Don't).* Jossey-Bass, 2013.

Susskind, Richard and Daniel Susskind. *The Future of the Professions: How Technology Will Transform the Work of Human Experts.* Oxford University Press, 2016.

Sutton, Robert I. *The No Asshole Rule: Building a Civilized Workplace and Surviving One That Isn't.* Business Plus, 2010.

Taleb, Nassim Nicholas. *The Black Swan: The Impact of the Highly Improbable.* Random House, 2007.

Tapscott, Don and Anthony D. Williams. *Radical Openness: Four Unexpected Principles for Success,* TED Conferences, 2013.

Tevelow, Jesse. *The Connection Algorithm: Take Risks, Defy the Status Quo, and Live Your Passions.* Amazon Digital Services, 2015.

Wright, Dana. *We've Got to START Meeting Like This!: Creating inspiring meetings, conferences, and events.* Amazon Digital Services, 2014.

NOTES

1   Eric Sinoway, *Howard's Gift*, Griffin, 2013.

2   Yuval Noah Harari, *Sapiens: A Brief History of Humankind*, Harper, 2015.

3   Robert D. Putnam, *Bowling Alone: The Collapse and Revival of American Community*, Simon & Schuster, 2000.

4   Dave Gray, *Liminal Thinking*.

5   Dave Gray, Sunni Brown, and James Macanufo, *Gamestorming: A Playbook for Innovators, Rulebreakers, and Changemakers*

6   Attributed to David Cooperrider of Case Western Reserve University.

7   Yuval Noah Harari, *Homo Deus: A Brief History of Tomorrow*, HarperCollins, 2017

8   Rolf Jensen, *The Dream Society: How the Coming Shift from Information to Imagination Will Transform Your Business*, McGraw-Hill, 1999.

9   William A. Gentry, Regina H. Eckert, Sarah A. Stawiski, and Sophia Zhao, *The Challenges Leaders Face Around the World*, Center for Creative Leadership, 2014.

10   Simon Sinek, "How great leaders inspire action," TED Talk, September 2009.

11   Klaus Schwab, *The Fourth Industrial Revolution*, Crown Business, 2017.

12   Harari, *Homo Deus*.

13   Jonah Lehrer, *Imagine: How Creativity Works,* Houghton Mifflin, 2012.

14   Don Tapscott and Anthony D. Williams, *Radical Openness: Four Unexpected Principles for Success,* TED Conferences, 2013.

15   Keith Ferrazzi. *Who's Got Your Back: The Breakthrough Program to Build Deep, Trusting Relationships That Create Success—and Won't Let You Fail,* Random House, 2009.

16   David H. Maister, Charles H. Green, and Robert M. Galford, *The Trusted Advisor,* Touchstone, 2001.

17   Michael J. Marquardt, *Leading with Questions: How Leaders Find the Right Solutions by Knowing What to Ask,* Jossey-Bass, 2014.

18   Schwab.

19   Greg McKeown, *Harvard Business Review,* "99% of Networking Is A Waste of Time," January 2015.

20   Tim Askew, *Inc.,* "Networking for People Who Hate Networking," February 17, 2015.

21   Ibid.

22   Bernadette Jiwa, *Difference: The one-page method for reimagining your business and reinventing your marketing,* CreateSpace, 2014.

23   See https://www.chathamhouse.org/about/chatham-house-rule.

CPSIA information can be obtained
at www.ICGtesting.com
Printed in the USA
BVHW062056230919
559228BV00004B/59/P